The Official
Manchester City
Football Club
Annual
2004

Written by
David Clayton

A Grange Publication

© 2003. Published by Grange Communications Ltd., Edinburgh,
under licence from Manchester City Football Club. Printed in the EU.

With thanks to Manchester City photographers, Edward Garvey and Thomas C Priskorn

ISBN 1-902704-62-2

£5.99

Contents

Page 5   Introduction

Page 6   2002/03 Season Review

Page 12   Season Stats

Page 14   Back in Europe!

Page 16   The KK Factor

Page 18   City Quiz

Page 19   Name Game Quiz

Page 21   Marc Vivien Foe

Page 22   City of Manchester Stadium

Page 28   Nicolas Anelka

Page 31   City Euro Quiz

Page 32   The French Connection

Page 34   True or False Quiz

Page 35   Who Said That Quiz

Page 36   Robbie Fowler – Back to Business

Page 48   Appearance Stats

Page 49   Who am I?

Page 51   Six Easy Points? City v. United

Page 52   The Last Game – The End of Maine Road

Page 56   Club History and Honours

Page 62   Answers

Introduction

Welcome to the Manchester City Annual 2004. In the following pages you will find all you need to know about the club and, hopefully, a few things you didn't know before. All the statistics are here including all the 2002/03 results and scorers plus each player's appearance details. There is a review of the season, a look at the squad and special features on Nicolas Anelka, Robbie Fowler and Kevin Keegan.

There is also information on City's new home at the City of Manchester Stadium and a last look at Maine Road, the club's home from 1923 until 2003. Add to that a feature entitled 'The French Connection', a look at last season's derby matches against Manchester United and a spotlight on the club's return to European football and there should be enough to keep you entertained for a while.

There are also plenty of questions to test on friends and family alike with the answers on pages 62 & 63 meaning you can be as cruel as you like in revealing the answers – knowledge is power!

City are set for an exciting season with a new stadium, European football and players such as David Seaman now at the club. We hope you enjoy the Manchester City Annual 2004

Season Review 2002/03

There was plenty of optimism amongst the travelling City fans for the opening day fixture at Elland Road. Terry Venables' Leeds United provided a stern test for the Division One champions who had Nicolas Anelka, Marc Vivien Foe and Sylvain Distin making their league debuts. Leeds rode their luck at times but were more clinical in front of goal and the 3-0 score line flattered them, somewhat.

Despite the opening day loss there had been much for Kevin Keegan to enthuse about and the visit of his old club Newcastle United presented another tough test for the Blues in their final season at Maine Road. Peter Schmeichel, originally believed to be out for eight weeks, made a stunning recovery to make his home debut and a scrambled goal from Darren Huckerby proved to be the winner in an entertaining clash. A deflected Darius Vassell goal was enough to give Aston Villa a 1-0 win but the Blues secured a 3-1 win over Everton with Anelka grabbing a couple of goals – his first for the club.

September was a largely disappointing month despite a spirited display at Arsenal. With City's goal coming from the head of Anelka (his first headed goal in England), the 2-1 defeat was no disgrace. Blackburn Rovers should have taken all three points after they led 2-0 at Maine Road and the home side was down to ten men (with ten minutes to go) following goals from David Thompson and Andy Cole. Anelka made it five goals in three games on 80 minutes to make it 2-1 and with seconds left, second half substitute Shaun Goater grabbed an injury time equaliser to lift the roof off Maine Road and earn his club an unlikely point. A fairly dull 0-0 draw at West Ham United was followed by a 3-0 home defeat to a Michael Owen-inspired Liverpool.

There was more disappointment as City capitulated on their first visit to the St Mary's Stadium where a rampant Southampton should have won by more than 2-0 and Chelsea added more woe to Keegan's side picking up their traditional three points at Maine Road in a 3-0 victory, with little Italian Gianfranco Zola outstanding.

An impressive 2-0 win at Birmingham City saw the Blues back to winning ways with goals from Jihai Sun and

Anelka and there was more success on the road with a 2-1 win at West Bromwich Albion a week later, with goals from Anelka and Goater.

The visit of Manchester United was to be the highlight of the season as City cruised home 3-1 with goals from Anelka and Goater, whose second decisive strike was also his hundredth for the Blues. Of all the wonderful memories from that

game, the look on Gary Neville's face after being outwitted by Goater will be one all City fans will cherish forever.

Despite the glory against the Reds, frustration was in the air as Charlton Athletic ended the run of league successes with a 1-0 win at Maine Road just one week later and Middlesbrough piled on more misery in a game when Shaun Wright-Phillips once again saw red, with Steve McClaren's side winning 3-1 and Anelka scoring the only

City goal. Steve Howey and Eyal Berkovic opened their Premiership accounts as City ended November with a 2-0 win over Bolton Wanderers. Progress was continued at the Stadium of Light ten days later in a 3-0 win at Sunderland. Goals from Marc Vivien Foe, Jihai Sun and a late effort from Goater pushed the Blues further up the Premiership table and an exciting 2-2 draw at Charlton four days was yet more proof that Keegan's side were coping well with life at the top with the ever-improving Foe scoring twice late on.

Tottenham Hotspur somehow left Maine Road with all three points, winning 3-2 after being out-played for much of the game. Howey and Benarbia scored for the Blues. There was far more to cheer on Boxing Day, three days later, as City turned on the style again and were this time rewarded with a 3-1 win against Aston Villa. Again Foe scored twice with Benarbia scoring the other. A 1-0 win at Fulham thanks to a late Anelka strike and a 2-2 draw at Everton saw further goals for Anelka and Foe and the Blues climbing the table rapidly.

The Blues then beat Leeds United 2-1 with goals from Goater and a wondrous volley from Niclas Jensen, but Newcastle United won 2-0 at St James' Park a week later with Alan Shearer scoring after just 10 seconds!

City were magnificent in the last senior night match to be played at Maine Road, winning 4-1 against Fulham with goals from Anelka, Benarbia, Foe and Wright-Phillips, yet doomed West Bromwich Albion ruined Robbie Fowler's debut with a surprise 2-1 win – even City's goal came courtesy of an own goal on a miserable afternoon in Moss Side. It was proving an up and down sort of season! Pride was restored a week

later as City gave Manchester United a fright in a 1-1 draw at Old Trafford with Goater again scoring against the Reds. Undoubtedly the worst day of the season came when Arsenal visited Maine Road for the last game of February and won 5-1 with Anelka grabbing a late consolation.

March had begun with a 1-0 defeat at Blackburn Rovers, followed by a 1-0 victory over Birmingham City, with Robbie Fowler scoring a memorable first goal in City colours. Defeats at Chelsea (5-0) and Bolton Wanderers (2-0) were followed by a 0-0 draw with Middlesbrough. The improvement continued with a polished 2-0

victory at Tottenham Hotspur where David Sommeil and Joey Barton scored their first goals for the club. Few would have guessed that the last City goal to ever be scored at Maine Road would be Foe's second strike in a 3-0 romp against Sunderland. Robbie Fowler got the other against the relegated Wearsiders.

Division One-bound West Ham United won the penultimate Maine Road match 1-0 before the Blues turned on the style

to win at Anfield for the first time since Boxing Day 1981. A double strike from former Reds' striker Anelka earned Keegan's men their most impressive away win of the season at Liverpool.

Finally, the day most City fans had dreaded arrived on May 11 with the visit of Southampton – the last fixture to be played at Maine Road. The visitors ruined the party with a 1-0 win but with City earning a place in UEFA Cup competition via the Fair Play League, it was a highly satisfying return to the top flight for all concerned with the club finishing in ninth place.

2002/03 season stats

Date	Versus	Score	Gate	Scorers
17	Leeds	0-3	40,195	
24	**Newcastle**	**1-0**	**34,776**	**Huckerby**
28	Aston Villa	0-1	33,494	
31	**Everton**	**3-1**	**34,835**	**Anelka (2), Radzinski (og)**
10	Arsenal	1-2	37,878	Anelka
15	**Blackburn**	**2-2**	**34,130**	**Anelka, Goater**
21	West Ham	0-0	35,050	
28	**Liverpool**	**0-3**	**35,141**	
01	**Crewe (WC 2)**	**3-2**	**21,820**	**Berkovic, Walker (og), Huckerby**
05	Southampton	0-2	31,009	
19	**Chelsea**	**0-3**	**34,953**	
26	Birmingham City	2-0	29,316	Sun, Anelka
02	West Brom	2-1	27,044	Anelka, Goater
05	Wigan Athletic (WC3)	0-1	15,007	
09	**Man United**	**3-1**	**34,649**	**Anelka, Goater (2)**
16	**Charlton Athletic**	**0-1**	**33,455**	
23	Middlesbrough	1-3	31,510	Anelka
30	**Bolton Wanderers**	**2-0**	**34,860**	**Howey, Berkovic**
09	Sunderland	3-0	36,511	Foe, Sun, Goater
14	Charlton Athletic	2-2	26,434	Foe (2)
23	**Tottenham**	**2-3**	**36,075**	**Howey, Benarbia**
26	**Aston Villa**	**3-1**	**33,991**	**Foe (2) Benarbia**
28	Fulham	1-0	17,937	Anelka
01	Everton	2-2	40,163	Anelka, Foe
05	**Liverpool (FA Cup 3)**	**0-1**	**28,586**	
11	**Leeds**	**2-1**	**34,884**	**Goater, Jensen**
18	Newcastle	0-2	52,152	
29	**Fulham**	**4-1**	**33,260**	**Anelka, Benarbia, Foe, Wright-Phillips**
01	**West Brom**	**1-2**	**34,765**	**Gilchrist (og)**
09	Man United	1-1	67,646	Goater
22	**Arsenal**	**1-5**	**34,960**	**Anelka**
01	Blackburn	0-1	28,647	
16	**Birmingham**	**1-0**	**34,596**	**Fowler**
22	Chelsea	0-5	41,105	
05	Bolton	0-2	26,949	
12	**Middlesbrough**	**0-0**	**34,793**	
18	Tottenham	2-0	36,500	Sommeil, Barton
21	Sunderland	3-0	34,357	Foe (2), Fowler
27	West Ham	0-1	34,815	
03	Liverpool	2-1	44,220	Anelka (2, 1 pen)
11	Southampton	0-1	34,957	

Home games in **BOLD**

1	Man United	38	16	2	1	42	12	9	6	4	32	22	83
2	Arsenal	38	15	2	2	47	20	8	7	4	38	22	78
3	Newcastle	38	15	2	2	36	17	6	4	9	27	31	69
4	Chelsea	38	12	5	2	41	15	7	5	7	27	23	67
5	Liverpool	38	9	8	2	30	16	9	2	8	31	25	64
6	Blackburn	38	9	7	3	24	15	7	5	7	28	28	60
7	Everton	38	11	5	3	28	19	6	3	10	20	30	59
8	Southampton	38	9	8	2	25	16	4	5	10	18	30	52
9	**Manchester City**	**38**	**9**	**2**	**8**	**28**	**26**	**6**	**4**	**9**	**19**	**28**	**51**
10	Tottenham	38	9	4	6	30	29	5	4	10	21	33	50
11	Middlesbrough	38	10	7	2	36	21	3	3	13	12	23	49
12	Charlton	38	8	3	8	26	30	6	4	9	19	26	49
13	Birmingham	38	8	5	6	25	23	5	4	10	16	26	48
14	Fulham	38	11	3	5	26	18	2	6	11	15	32	48
15	Leeds	38	7	3	9	25	26	7	2	10	33	31	47
16	Aston Villa	38	11	2	6	25	14	1	7	11	17	33	45
17	Bolton	38	7	8	4	27	24	3	6	10	14	27	44
18	West Ham	38	5	7	7	21	24	5	5	9	21	35	42
19	West Brom	38	3	5	11	17	34	3	3	13	12	31	26
20	Sunderland	38	3	2	14	11	31	1	5	13	10	34	19

Back in Europe!

City ended their 24-year absence from European football after they qualified for the UEFA Cup via the Fair Play League. Kevin Keegan had boldly predicted European football was possible at the start of last season and though entry was gained by the 'back door' so to speak, it has excited fans and players alike at the prospect of hosting some of Europe's top clubs again.

The Fair Play League has been in operation for several years now and Ipswich Town were the beneficiaries of a similar award last season. Yet the Manchester Blues didn't even finish top of the English Fair Play table – they were behind Manchester United, Liverpool, Chelsea, Newcastle and Blackburn Rovers – all of whom had already qualified for Europe through more conventional routes.

With City being the next highest placed club in the list, they needed to finish higher in the Premiership than their nearest rivals Middlesbrough to guarantee a spot and then hope England topped the Fair Play table for Europe. All this happened, so it was quite a complicated entry when all is told!

The Blues were paired with Welsh non-league side Total Network Solutions in the first qualifying round. This was also the first competitive game to be played in the City of Manchester Stadium – quite an honour for a side that attracts just 200 fans to its home ground in Treflan, mid-Wales. The return game was played at the Millennium Stadium in Cardiff – City's first visit to the temporary home of the FA & League Cup finals.

City may have been absent from the European circuit for almost a quarter of a century, but they have certainly made their mark in the past. The last UEFA Cup venture ended with defeat in the quarterfinals against German side Borussia Monchengladbach, but the Blues had already demolished AC Milan and Standard Liege along the way.

Previous campaigns saw City beat Juventus 1-0 at Maine Road before losing the return leg 2-0 and a narrow defeat to Fenerbahce in the Blues' only ever European Cup tie in 1968. The following year City became the first English team to win a European trophy and a domestic cup in the same season.

They won through to the final of the European Cup Winners' Cup and played Polish side Gornik Zabrze in Austria. Because of travel problems for the Gornik side and the distance and time of the match (an evening kick-off), around 10,000 watched the match on an appallingly wet Vienna night. City won 2-1 with goals from Francis Lee and Neil Young.

The Blues almost repeated the feat the following year but drew Chelsea in the semi-finals of the same competition. The Pensioners won both legs 1-0 and remain the only side to have beaten City at home in European football.

If City can negotiate the first few rounds successfully, they will face the cream of Europe from the fourth round. It should be an exciting season for the Blues who will be looking to finish high enough this season to guarantee European football is not just a one-off and is here to stay.

15

The KK Factor

When City appointed Kevin Keegan as the new manager in June 2001, few could have of imagined the dramatic effect he would have in his first two seasons in charge. The Blues had been relegated and taken the decision to part company with Joe Royle and were facing an uncertain future.

There was hardly time to begin wondering who the new man might be before the club called a Press conference to announce that Keegan was in charge at Maine Road. Looking refreshed and raring to go after his spell as England manager, one of the most famous men in football history set about returning the Blues to their rightful place amongst the nation's elite.

Top-name players such as Stuart Pearce and Eyal Berkovic were soon signed to bolster the squad's chances of an immediate return to the Premiership. It quickly became clear that the name of Kevin Keegan alone was enough to attract some of the best players in the game.

His first match in charge was a Saturday evening kick-off against Watford and Maine Road crackled with an electric, turbo-charged atmosphere of expectancy and excitement. The subsequent manner in which City beat Watford 3-0 suggested there would be many happy days ahead under Keegan's tenure.

His ability to attract the best was again demonstrated later that season when he signed former French player of the year Ali Benarbia on a free transfer and the Algerian's impact was amazing, inspiring his new team mates to some wonderful displays. By the end of his first season, Kevin Keegan had restored City's reputation of being an attacking football side intent on winning matches with style and panache.

They were also runaway champions of Division One, ending the season with over one hundred goals and breaking several club records along the way. During the summer break, even bigger names arrived at the club. Peter Schmeichel, Sylvain Distin, Marc Vivien Foe and, perhaps the biggest of them all, Nicolas Anelka were all now wearing Laser Blue and to a man they cited Keegan as the biggest influencing factor in their move to Manchester.

The Blues soon settled to life amongst the elite of English football but for the first time in a decade, they actually looked as though they may challenge in the top half of the table as opposed to scrapping out a fight against relegation with eight or so other clubs. There were highs and lows in the first half of the season but the 3-1 victory over Manchester United in the last-ever Maine Road derby created emotions that were impossible to pigeon-hole. City continued to impress in bursts but disappoint, too, on occasions.

Robbie Fowler became the latest household name to join City at the turn of the year after Keegan had personally become involved in the transfer negotiations. Even more big names were to follow in the months ahead.

Heavy losses against Chelsea and Arsenal were followed by an impressive win at one of Keegan's former clubs Liverpool and it was that win that would enable the Blues to finish ninth in the table – quite an achievement. Thanks to the club's disciplinary record, they earned a place in the UEFA Cup via the Fair Play League.

David Seaman and Michael Tarnat couldn't resist the opportunity of working with the City boss who is incredibly popular with both players and supporters because of his open, honest personality and enthusiasm to play the game the way it should be played. To have achieved what he has in just two

seasons – promotion and a top-ten finish - is a testament to his ability as a manager and as he begins his third season in charge of the Blues it's hard to imagine a man better suited to being boss of Manchester City FC. King Kevin - long may he reign.

City Quiz

1. Who was the only City player to score in both Manchester derby games last season?

2. Which team did Robbie Fowler score his first goal for City against?

3. Which other English teams has Eyal Berkovic played for?

4. Which current City player used to play for Real Madrid?

5. Name the City player who went on loan to Nottingham Forest last season.

6. Name the City player who retired from international football with Northern Ireland last season.

7. Who was the last City player to score at Maine Road?

8. Who knocked City out of last season's Worthington Cup?

9. City's Under-17 & Under-19 sides both won their leagues last season – true or false?

10. Who was the reserves' top scorer last season?

Name Game

How good are you at anagrams? If you think you are pretty good, re-arrange the letters of the words below to make the name of a current City player. You'll need a piece of paper, a pen and a little bit of patience to solve them all!

1. LIVE ROCK A BYE

2. INSANE KOALA CO

3. A MAD SAVE DIN

4. YEAR NOT JOB

5. ARABIA BE NIL

6. A CHARM AIL TENT

7. AND IN A TOTTY

8. MILD SAM VIDEO

9. U HOPE A PLAN COW

10. BELOW FIR BORE

Marc Vivien Foe
The Gentle Giant

Marc Vivien Foe signed for City following the 2002 World Cup in Japan and Korea. The Cameroon midfielder had been in impressive form for the Indomitable Lions and his addition to the Blues' engine room was a welcome boost to the Club's return to the Premiership. The Blues paid £500,000 for his services and it would prove to be money extremely well spent. The tall, tough-tackling ball-winner chose the No.23 shirt as his squad number and made his debut in the 3-0 opening-day defeat to Leeds United.

In the following months he became an important member of the first team and opened his scoring account for the Club against Sunderland in December. It was the beginning of a prolific run of goals with six strikes coming within the space of just 23 days. His presence had become a driving force in midfield and his contribution was enormous; however he always went about his job quietly, and for a hard man on the pitch, there were no face-to-face incidents with players from opposing clubs. He fought hard but fairly and was respected by his fellow professionals.

His scoring continued, but he never sought the limelight and when he was interviewed he was keen to thank his team-mates' contribution and the backing of the City fans– supporters he felt were amazing in their unswerving loyalty. He found the net again when City played Sunderland on April 21st, but few realised that it would be the last goal ever scored at Maine Road, especially with two more home games to come.

By the end of the season he had scored nine goals and finished second top scorer after Nicolas Anelka – quite a feat for a defensive midfielder and one that had won him an army of new fans at Maine Road. His popularity was often aired with the chant of 'Come on feed the Foe' – a variation of a Shaun Goater song.

Most expected City to make the deal permanent once the season finished, but his French club Lyon, were demanding a fee of around £7million, which was felt to be unrealistic in the transfer climate at that time. Eventually, Lyon indicated that Foe could leave on a free transfer and it seemed the move to Manchester would at last become a permanent one. Negotiations were on-going and despite interest from several other Premiership clubs, Foe's most likely destination was the club he had just spent a year on loan to.

The Confederations Cup began in France in June and Foe, wearing the No.17 shirt he always wore for his country, was instrumental in the Indomitable Lions reaching the semi-final. He took to the field for Cameroon against Colombia and during the game, tragically collapsed and died shortly after. Investigations revealed his untimely death was due to natural causes, but for the world of football and City fans in particular, it was unbelievable that this fit, powerful 28 year-old man should suffer such a fate.

Tributes poured in from around the world and City's old ground Maine Road became a shrine of flowers, flags, scarves and shirts from all over Britain and beyond. Marc Vivien Foe was a much-loved man and a highly respected footballer. The Club removed his No.23 shirt as a permanent mark of respect and further tributes are planned. A moving memorial service at Manchester Cathedral was held in Marc's memory and was attended by Club staff and fans alike.

His presence both on and off the pitch will be sorely missed.

The Pride of
Manchester

Manchester City begin the 2003/04 season in their new home, the City of Manchester Stadium after 80 years at their old ground Maine Road. The 48,000-capacity arena cost in the region of £130 million to build and was first used for the 2002 Commonwealth Games as an athletics stadium.

With the Manchester skyline clearly visible to the west, there isn't a Premiership club in the country – or most of Europe - that can match the design and facilities available for the club and supporters at the City of Manchester Stadium. It will surely inspire Kevin Keegan's men to great things in the coming years with the noise level alone scaring the pants off many visiting teams. With the new stadium designed to keep noise in, Blue Moon will never have sounded so good.

There will be 36,000 season-ticket holders this season – an increase of around 10,000 from last season and virtually guaranteeing a full-house for every Premiership fixture. There are 68 hospitality boxes, six restaurants and several luxurious suites including the magnificent 'Legends Lounge' that will incorporate a Hall of Fame and is located in the South Stand.

Giant shutters will be opened around the ground before and after matches for ventilation that is vital for the pitch condition and ramps, rather than stairs, will allow safe access and egress from the stands making for a gentle descent after the match rather than the mad rush to exit down staircases that still exist at many football grounds in this country.

The ticket office is situated within the North Stand and the new CityStore will be located in ReebokCity close to the North Stand on the Northern Plaza but will be three times bigger in size than the old superstore and will also house a bar and restaurant plus the Heritage Centre on another level.

The disabled facilities and seating areas are second-to-none and the stadium boasts more first aid rooms than any other ground in the country. The new Family Stand is bigger and takes up three blocks behind the goal on the lower tier of the North Stand.

The home and away team changing rooms are fitted out to the highest standard and there is a warm-up room for the players if they need to use it. There is also a crèche for the players' children to use on match days. The dug-outs will be slightly raised and set-back a little but the manager will still have a covered area actually on the sidelines.

A walk down the players' tunnel sends shivers down the spine and it will not be hard for the manager to inspire his team to perform on this magnificent stage and for a while, every game is going to feel like a cup final. The sophisticated lighting around the stadium roof will make night matches feel like day and internationals, concerts and semi-finals will all be held at the ground in the future.

It will be, after all, Britain's premier sports stadium.

Nico – Home At Last

Nicolas Anelka became City's record signing when he put pen to paper on a deal that cost the Blues £13.5million in June 2002. He had been playing for most of the previous season on loan at Liverpool and it was widely expected that the French international would join the Reds on a permanent basis. However, Anfield boss Gerard Houllier decided not to buy Anelka and Kevin Keegan moved quickly to secure his services from Paris St Germain.

A product of Clairefontaine School of Excellence (which also included Thierry Henry), Anelka began club life as a junior at PSG and broke into the first team aged 16, making his debut against Monaco and playing just ten games before Arsenal boss Arsene Wenger paid £500,000 for the unknown 17 year-old in February 1997.

'Nico' made his debut three months later in a 3-0 victory over Chelsea but it was the next season when he began to establish himself in the first team and became a vital member of the side that pipped Manchester United to the Premiership title and then

scored the second decisive goal in the 2-0 FA Cup final victory over Newcastle United.

He was not, however, included in the triumphant 1998 French squad that went on to lift the World Cup. The 1998/99 campaign saw Anelka really take off as he settled into the English pace and he capped a magnificent season with the Gunners by being voted PFA Young Player of the Year and also scored one of the goals that secured a 2-0 win against England at Wembley.

He then moved to Real Madrid for a world record fee of £23million. He also took part in Euro 2000 and played every game except the final when his country was crowned European champions.

After a relatively unhappy year in Spain he returned to his

homeland to play for his first club PSG. The fee? £22million! After just one season he was loaned to Liverpool and eventually ended up at Manchester City. His transfer to Maine Road meant he had been involved in deals worth an incredible £59million!

With the media spotlight in Manchester far less intense than at any of his previous clubs, Anelka could at last enjoy a walk down the street in peace without a pack of photographers chasing him and he soon settled and began playing the kind of football that had made him one of the most famous footballers in the world.

He freely admits he is very happy at City and has the respect of the manager, team-mates and supporters. He is a polite, quiet young man who is idolised by the younger City fans and has had a successful first season with the Blues, finishing top scorer with 14 goals and playing in every game. It seems that, at last, he has found a home to concentrate on doing what he does best – playing football.

City in Europe Quiz

1. Which English team did City meet in the 1971 European Cup Winners' Cup semi-final and what was the final aggregate score?

2. City were the first English club to win a major European Cup competition and win a domestic trophy in the same season – true or false?

3. Which team have City met most often in Europe and how many games have there been?

4. How many Italian sides have City played in Europe and who are they?

5. City have never lost a UEFA Cup tie at home – true or false?

6. What honour did Welsh side Total Network Solutions have when they met City in the UEFA Cup this season?

7. Name the three managers to lead City in Europe.

8. How many French sides have City played in Europe?

9. Which part-time team from Northern Ireland almost knocked the Blues out in the 1970/71 European Cup Winners' Cup competition?

10. Who scored the last European goal for City at Maine Road?

The French Connection

Manchester City's 'French Connection' began when Joe Royle signed Laurent Charvet from Newcastle United for £2million in 2000 making the defender the first player from across the Channel to represent the Blues in 113 years of existence. Charvet's stay at the club was largely disappointing but when new manager Kevin Keegan took over at Maine Road, he targeted France as a key supplier of affordable talent for his squad.

Lucien Mettomo, a Cameroon international was signed from Bordeaux and was followed by striker Alioune Toure from Paris St Germain for £500,000. His next signing, again from PSG, was also one of his best – Ali Benarbia. Raised in the French coastal town of Martigues, the Algerian-born playmaker had been named French Player of the Year on two occasions and was available on a free transfer from PSG. He travelled to Sunderland to meet Peter Reid but was disappointed to be only offered a trial. He stopped at Carrington on his way back home to meet his friend Toure and ended up having lunch – and agreeing a two-year deal – with Kevin Keegan!

Benarbia's influence was one of the main reasons City walked away with the Division One title in 2001/02. After a successful year in the Premiership Benarbia decided to leave the club. Also signed that season was French colonist Christian Negouai who was playing his football at Belgian side Charleroi for a fee of £2 million.

There were still more players with links to France to come. For the start of the 2002/03 Sylvain Distin was bought from PSG for a fee of £4 million after he failed to sign for Newcastle United with whom he'd spent a year on loan with during 2001/02. Then French international superstar Nicolas Anelka joined the Blues for a fee of £13.5 million from – yet again – Paris St Germain. The deal smashed City's transfer record by some £9 million and the former Arsenal and Real Madrid player went on to be top scorer for his new club in season 2002/03 after notching 14 goals. Also signed on loan was Cameroon midfielder Marc Vivien Foe. The Lyon star played in almost every game of the 2002/03 campaign and finished second top scorer with nine goals. Many expected the deal to become

permanent after the loan spell ended but Foe tragically died whilst playing for his country in the Confederations Cup.

Djamel Belmadi and Karim Kerkar – both Algerians playing in France were signed on loan but failed to impress the City boss enough into making the deals permanent. The final French connected player to sign for City was David Sommeil. The Bordeaux defender cost Keegan £3.5 million and quickly formed a good understanding with compatriot Distin in the heart of the City defence. To date, the Blues have paid around £27 million for French connected talent with the likelihood that there will be more to follow.

True or False

1. Kevin Keegan once had a top 20 hit called 'Head Over Heels in Love'. True/False?

2. Shaun Goater scored on his debut for Manchester United against Leicester City in 1989. True/False?

3. The last game at Maine Road and the first official game at the City of Manchester were both against teams nicknamed 'The Saints'. True/False?

4. Sylvain Distin has never scored a goal in England. True/False?

5. City's ninth place finish in season 2002/03 was the club's highest ever placing in the Premiership. True/False?

6. Nicolas Anelka has only ever played for teams who play in the same colours of his country – red, white and blue. True/False?

7. Shaun Goater, David Seaman, & Robbie Fowler all have MBE's. True/False?

8. City hold the record English attendance for a match played outside London. True/False?

9. Nicky Weaver had only played one league game for Mansfield Town when City signed him in 1996. True/False?

10. Jihai Sun played for Wimbledon FC in 1998/99. True/False?

Who said that?

Think you know the City players well? Then try and work out who made the quotes below during last season. The clues are in the quotes…

1   "I give one hundred per cent in training to keep my fitness because it is such a big part of my game. I like to see as much as I can of the ball as possible during a game and keep moving around the pitch for ninety minutes."

2   "Sometimes it's nice to be kept on your toes by your team-mates. As a manager or as a player I don't think it's nice if they have to have a real go at somebody, even if they've earned it. Some players need an arm around their shoulder and some need a volley and it's important you know what suits whom best. Everybody is different."

3   "A lot of people have said they hoped I would carry on and for them to say that means I am probably going out at just the right time."

4   "I'm just happy to be here and I want to work hard for Manchester City. I think about the club first. If everything is good here, the rest will follow. If I do get called up by France, I am ready."

5   "At Arsenal I wanted to show people how much I cared. But maybe I did it in the wrong way as I wanted to be on the pitch at the end to help us get an equaliser."

6   "I saw a lot of Manchester City fans before the game. It was nice because I was in Japan and you don't expect to see City fans out there but they were very supportive and it was a great boost for me at the time."

7   "It makes me feel good when I hear the City fans sing my name. I know that they like me and sometimes when I a bit down and missing home I hear the City fans and I forget about my problems."

8   "Kevin came to my house and told me all about the ambitions of the club. From what he had to say, I was very impressed."

9   "I am enjoying playing for City, but we all know we need to improve. I feel very settled and the supporters have been behind me from the very first game, which I appreciate a lot."

10   "I must admit, I felt as though I'd played my last game for the club when I was suspended and waiting to be sacked. I was just thinking: what's next?"

Robbie Fowler: Back to Business

Robbie Fowler joined City hoping to re-discover the form that just a few years ago made him the hottest property in British football. He signed from Leeds United where he suffered a serious hip injury and his career came to an abrupt halt. There were concerns whether he would play again at one point, but thankfully, he battled his way back and was given the all-clear to begin training again.

He became one of a series of huge stars to leave the Yorkshire club when City made a firm offer to secure his services after the transfer window re-opened in January 2003.

Fowler agreed to join the Blues but dramatically changed his mind at the last moment. Kevin Keegan was disappointed not to get his man but felt that perhaps not all had been done to convince Fowler that his future lay on the west side of the Pennines. Keegan made a personal visit to Fowler's Merseyside apartment and a few days later, the 27 year-old striker had signed for City in a deal worth £5.5million – a very reasonable fee considering Fowler's past history.

The Toxteth-born predator joined Liverpool aged 11 and went on to score an incredible 171 goals in 330 appearances for the Reds including five on his full home debut against Fulham in September 1993. He effectively became Ian Rush's replacement and soon won his first England U-21 cap, scoring after just 3 minutes on his debut.

In 1995/96 he bagged 36 goals in all competitions and was also voted the PFA Young Player of the Year by his fellow professionals. His first full England cap followed shortly after and he has – to date – won 26 in total. He holds the record for the fastest Premiership hat-trick – 4 minutes and 32 seconds – for the treble he scored against Arsenal. His last goals for Liverpool were, typically, a hat-trick against Leicester City in October 2001.

He then joined Leeds United shortly after for £11 million and his stay in Yorkshire began with six goals in his first eight games but his time there was blighted by a hip injury and he played just 30 times for the Lillywhites, scoring 16 goals in the process. Though he was passed fit to play again, he found himself on the Leeds bench more often than not and his hopes of regaining full match fitness seemed a distant dream under Terry Venables.

He came on as substitute in the Premiership fixture with City in early January and received a tremendous ovation from the City fans who clearly believed he was on his way to Maine Road! They were, of course, correct in their assumption and Fowler made his debut in a 2-1 home defeat to West Brom and finally opened his account for his new club against Birmingham City five matches later with a spectacular volley.

Like his strike partner Nicolas Anelka, he has chosen Manchester City to restore his reputation as one of the most lethal strikers in Europe. If he gets anywhere near his best, Keegan will have made one of the most astute signings in the club's history.

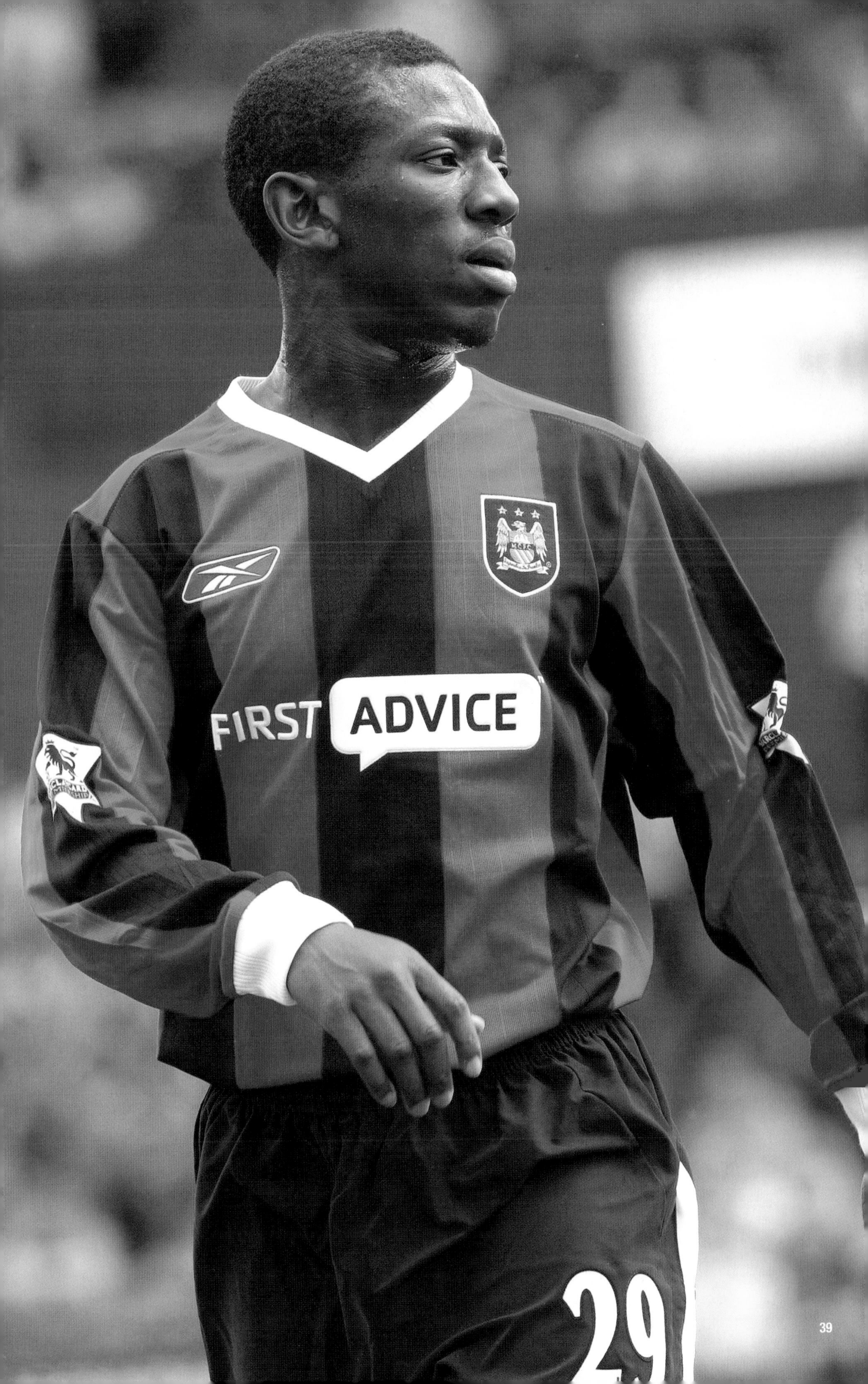
FIRST ADVICE
29

Player Profiles

David Seaman

Capped 72 times by his country, David Seaman joined City after 13 years with Arsenal and has clocked up more than 1,000 appearances in his long, distinguished career. He takes over from retiring Dane Peter Schmeichel and City fans will hope he has a similar impact. At 39 years old, he is hoping to inspire his new club to at least one trophy and is keen to prove Arsenal were wrong in allowing him to leave.

Carlo Nash

Set for a second spell on the sidelines after being number two to Schmeichel during season 2002/03. Now in his fourth year with the club, he will be looking to grasp the chance to reclaim the first choice spot should Seaman be forced to miss any matches. A good, reliable goalkeeper.

Nick Weaver

Injured for most of the past two seasons but despite being only 24 years-old, he is one of the club's longest-serving players, now in his eighth season with the club. Once he is fully fit he will challenge Seaman and Nash for the top spot and when he is at the top of his game, he is one of the best young goalkeepers in the country.

Richard Dunne

Slimmed down, he played for much of the second half of the season, though often out of his favoured central defensive position. Faces stiff competition to play in the middle but has the talent to achieve anything he wants.

Danny Tiatto

City's firebrand utility star, the Australian international is also one of the most popular players at the club. Signed five years ago as a squad player he became a first team regular with a series of totally committed displays that endeared him to the City fans' hearts. A short fuse has threatened his City career on more than one occasion and a number of red cards had interrupted his progress but his skill and endeavour make him almost an automatic choice when fit.

David Sommeil

Sommeil joined City from Bordeaux in January 2003 for £3.5million. He took time to settle in the side but ended the last campaign looking solid and assured in a back four formation. Quick and fierce in the tackle, his partnership with Sylvain Distin helped the Blues end the season as one of the meanest defences in England.

Player Profiles

Sylvain Distin

A thoroughbred defender who towers over most opposition attackers yet hardly relies at all on aerial advantage. His speed and ability to read situations make him a tough prospect for opposing forwards and his consistent level of performances throughout his first season with City made him many fans' personal player of the year. Costing £4million from PSG he represents money extremely well spent.

Jihai Sun

Played in around two thirds of City's matches last season but found himself on the bench for the last few months, Jihai Sun has made the transition from Chinese football to the Premiership in impressive fashion. Likely to be more of a squad player than a first-team regular for the start of the new season. Energetic and whole-hearted, he is a useful addition to any side.

Mikkel Bischoff

Classy young Danish U-21 defender who would possibly have been given a sustained first team run but for an unfortunate injury midway through last season. Made an impressive debut against Blackburn Rovers and looks set for a promising future with the Blues and many believe he will be hard to shift when his chance eventually comes.

Lucien Mettomo

Only played five games last season and unfortunate not to play more often. System and tactical changes have also restricted the Cameroon international's involvement but he looked in fantastic form in the 2003 Confederations Cup for his country. A talented defender who may yet force his way back into the first team.

Kevin Horlock

In his eighth season with Manchester City, Kevin Horlock has played more than 200 games for the club and is now the longest-serving player on the club's books. His role within the side has changed from the creative midfielder to defensive anchor behind the likes of Eyal Berkovic and Ali Benarbia. Seems content to play his new part in Keegan's side but his passing ability and accuracy with the dead-ball remain amongst the best at the club.

Eyal Berkovic

Once described as 'the beating heart of the City team', Berkovic has been one of the Blues' most influential players over the past two campaigns. His starring role in both Manchester derbies proved his class and ability was amongst the best in Europe and the man, known as 'the magician' in his homeland of Israel, has turned in more than a few tricks in his time with the Blues. Wonderful vision and skill on the ball, Berkovic is the type of player all football fans love to watch.

Player Profiles

Trevor Sinclair

England international winger Trevor Sinclair joined City in late July for a fee of £2.5million from relegated West Ham United. He signed a four-year deal with the Blues and will be keen to rediscover the form that made him one the hottest properties in English football a few years ago. Born in London and raised in Manchester, he made his name firstly at Blackpool and then QPR before moving to Upton Park.

Joe Barton

Promoted from the reserves following several poor performances by the first team squad, Barton made a huge impact on his debut at Bolton and continued in the same vein for the remainder of the season. He promised to make it impossible for the manager to drop him once he was given a chance and, so far, has been true to his word. Tough-tackling with plenty of ability, Barton was the discovery of last season and will be keen to progress further in 2003/04.

Shaun Wright-Phillips

Ended last season one short of a hundred appearances for City and has played in virtually every position during that time. He seems comfortable in any role but attacking midfield appears to be his favourite. His dribbling skill and ability to take on and beat defenders is at its most potent when playing in a forward role. A real gem of a player and a manager's dream both on and off the pitch.

Michael Tarnat

Signed in the summer on a free transfer from Bayern Munich, Tarnat has represented Germany more than fifty times and is one of the country's most respected players. He can play either as a full-back or as a defensive midfielder and will bring much-needed steel and experience to the Blues in season 2003/04.

Jon Macken

Unfortunate with injury since his £5million move from Preston North End, Macken has shown enough to suggest that, given a sustained run in the side, he will offer another attacking option for Keegan, should he require it. The ex-Manchester United youngster will need instant results when a chance does present itself if he is to claim a berth up front on a more permanent basis.

Paulo Wanchope

Almost the forgotten man of Manchester City, Wanchope injured his knee and missed the whole of the 2002/03 season and last played for the Blues in February 2002. After prolonged treatment, he finally began training towards the end of last season only to injure his shoulder and miss the remainder of the campaign. With just 42 appearances in three years with the Blues, he has a lot of catching up to do but has wonderful ability and should feature prominently this season.

Player Profiles

Gerard Wiekens

Now one of the longest-serving players at the club, Gerard Wiekens underlined his value to the squad by marking Ruud van Nistelrooy out of the Maine Road Manchester derby. He was unfortunate to fall ill shortly after and with severe competition in the heart of the City defence, he was limited to just a handful of appearances for the remainder of the campaign. Dependable whenever called upon.

Christian Negouai

Injury kept him out of the 2002/03 campaign but with his problems behind him he has shown enough in pre-season matches to suggest he will be a vital addition to the Blues' engine room. Standing at 6 feet 4 inches, he cuts an imposing figure on the pitch and will be keen to kick-start his career with the club once again.

Robbie Fowler

Finally signed for City in January 2003 after a drawn-out transfer saga with Leeds United. Played a dozen games towards the end of last season and showed glimpses of the form that made him the hottest property in English football a few years back. Scored a couple of goals and will have benefited from a few full games under his belt, plus a close season training programme designed to help him rediscover his match sharpness.

Nicolas Anelka

City's record signing and a crowd idol for the young supporters, Anelka is probably the first name on Kevin Keegan's team sheet. Played in every game for the Blues last season and finished top scorer with 14 goals, he has proved that he is still amongst the best strikers in the world. Suffered from the lack of a regular partner for much of the campaign, Anelka's all-round work-rate has made him a firm favourite with the City faithful.

Paul Bosvelt

Dutch international midfielder Paul Bosvelt became one of Kevin Keegan's summer signings when he joined the Blues for an undisclosed fee. He left Feyenoord after six seasons, captaining them to the UEFA Cup glory in 2002. With 18 caps for Holland and a reputation as a tough-tackling powerhouse of a player, he is set to become a firm favourite during the 2003/04 season.

Antoine Sibierski

French midfield playmaker Antoine Sibierski signed for the Blues in early August in a deal worth £700,000. He joined City from French club Lens and has played for Lille, Auxerre and Nantes during his career. He has also represented his country in the 1996 Olympics and brings a wealth of Champions League and UEFA Cup experience with him and will fill a creative void left by the departing Ali Benarbia.

Appearance Stats

No	Name	League & Cup Record 2002/03		City Career	
		Apps	Goals	Apps	Goals
1	Peter Schmeichel	31	0	31	0
20	Carlo Nash	10	0	40 (1)	0
2	David Sommeil	14	1	14	1
3	Niclas Jensen	35(1)	1	53 (2)	2
4	Gerard Wiekens	6(2)	0	194 (15)	10
5	Sylvain Distin	36	0	36	0
17	Jihai Sun	28(3)	2	30 (8)	2
22	Richard Dunne	25(1)	0	99 (4)	1
24	Steve Howey	26	2	103	11
25	Lucien Mettomo	5(1)	0	23 (8)	1
27	Mikkel Bischoff	1	0	1	0
6	Kevin Horlock	24(9)	0	212 (20)	42
19	Danny Tiatto	10(3)	0	125 (25)	4
23	Marc Vivien Foe	38	9	38	9
31	Djamel Belmadi	2(6)	0	2 (6)	0
41	Joe Barton	7	1	7	1
8	Ali Benarbia	24(12)	3	66 (12)	11
14	Eyal Berkovic	28(1)	2	53 (7)	9
29	Shaun Wright-Phillips	25(9)	1	74 (25)	9
44	Chris Shuker	1(2)	0	1 (5)	1
10	Shaun Goater	16(13)	7	189 (23)	103
11	Jonathan Macken	0 (5)	0	4 (9)	5
36	Robbie Fowler	12(1)	2	12 (1)	2
39	Nicolas Anelka	41	14	41	14

Substitute appearances in brackets

Who am I?

All the clues below relate to current City players – see if you can figure out who they are…

1. I was born in Rotherham in 1963 but my first club, Leeds United, rejected me as a youngster. I went on to play for Birmingham City and Peterborough United before moving to QPR. From there I moved to Arsenal for £1.3 million. Who am I?

2. I am a striker who has scored a goal against Brazil but first made my name for Derby County, scoring a wonderful solo goal at Old Trafford in my first season. I left Derby County for West Ham United before joining City. Who am I?

3. I began life at Manchester United but never played for the first team. From there I moved north to a lower league side and it was there I made my name. My best ever goal came against City and I scored again for my old club in the return match. I joined the Blues and then scored a goal that equalled a record. Who am I?

4. I began life in the Burnley amateur leagues before being signed by Crystal Palace. From there I moved north to Stockport County. I then signed for City for £100,000 and conceded four goals in the first twenty minutes of my home debut. Who am I?

5. I was rejected by Nottingham Forest as a teenager but moved to City where I progressed from youth team to first team. I scored my first Premiership goal against Fulham last season and have appeared on This Is Your Life. Who am I?

6. My first English club was Southampton and from there I moved to West Ham United. I then moved to Scotland to play for my next team before joining City for £1.5million and scoring on my debut. Who am I?

7. My first club was Mansfield Town and I joined City as a teenager. I have played at Wembley and won several England Under-21 caps over the years but have missed most of the last couple of seasons with injury. Who am I?

8. I was raised in France but have played international football for an African country. I have been named footballer of the year twice in France and have played in the Champions League. I was also voted player of the year at City in my first season. Who am I?

9. I have played in France and Spain before I joined City. I played in every game during the 2002/03 season and scored the only penalty the Blues were awarded last season. My first ever headed goal in England came at one of my former clubs. Who am I?

10. I have played in midfield with Kinkladze, Bishop and Berkovic. I was born in England but played my international football for another country and I have twice scored for City at Wembley. Who am I?

City v United 2002/03

City's promotion back to the Premiership brought some familiar responses from Manchester United supporters. Most were happy that the Manchester derby would be taking place again but the general feeling amongst the Reds' fans was that playing City represented nothing more than 'six easy points'.

Infuriating though these comments may have been, who could blame United fans for teasing their deadly rivals? The Blues had failed miserably home and away against United for more than a decade with the last victory being the famous 5-1 win in September 1989.

City's record at Old Trafford was even worse with the last win being as far back as 1974 when Denis Law's cheeky back-heel confirmed his former club's relegation. There was added spice to the first derby of the 2002/03 season because it was also the last ever at Maine Road and City fans were demanding nothing less than a win.

The Blues had lost both Steve Howey and Sylvain Distin with injury allowing Gerard Wiekens and Lucien Mettomo to make their first appearances of the season. Straight from the kick-off it was clear that City were up for this match and Nicolas Anelka scored inside ten minutes to give the Blues the lead but United levelled a couple of minutes later through Ole Gunnar Solskjaer.

With the game evenly poised Gary Neville attempted to allow a poor Mettomo pass to run out of play but Shaun Goater refused to give it up and nicked the ball away from Neville before sliding a perfect shot past Fabien Barthez for 2-1. Neville looked to the heavens but there was no hiding place as the City fans taunted him mercilessly. With Berkovic and Wiekens particularly outstanding, the Blues could and should have added to their lead before the break.

Minutes after half-time, Berkovic fed Goater who coolly chipped the ball over Barthez for 3-1 – it was also Goater's one hundredth goal for City – what a time to get it! United couldn't get back in the game and the 3-1 result gave the Maine Road fans exactly the win they had dreamed of.

The return game at Old Trafford with United represented a chance for the Reds to avenge the Maine Road defeat and with David Beckham and Roy Keane back in the side, they were at full strength and pushing for the top spot. In fact, many believed it was defeat by City that fuelled United's dramatic improvement in form. United went 1-0 up and they should have increased the lead in the second half but for some brave defending from Distin.

With four minutes to go, Shaun Goater and Ali Benarbia were brought on as City prepared to take a free-kick on the edge of the United box. Benarbia touched it to Wright-Phillips who chipped the ball to the far post for Goater to power a header home with his first touch of the ball. Minutes later, the ball crashed against the United bar and fell to Anelka who squared it for Goater to put in the back of the net.

The referee had seen the ball strike Anelka's hand and the goal was ruled out. A draw overall was a fair result but the Blues, once again inspired by Eyal Berkovic, finished by far the better team. The draw meant the Blues had taken four of the six points available giving City fans the rare chance to thank their United counterparts for the 'four easy points'! The 2002/03 derby honours most definitely went to the blue half of the city.

The Last Game

May 11, 2003
City 0, Southampton 1

The Blues played their last-ever home game at Maine Road against Southampton last May but they failed to make the events on the pitch memorable with a below-par display. The Saints scored the only goal of the game through Michael Svensson on 34 minutes.

A crowd of 34,957 had crammed into the ground to witness the day's events which began with a parade of former legends. Then it was down to action for Kevin Keegan's men but despite Southampton's involvement in the FA Cup final the following week, the visitors proved to be stubborn and focused on finishing higher in the table than City.

Considering all the fantastic matches and occasions that the old stadium had played host to, the defeat left most supporters feeling a little flat. There was a tremendous reception for the team for their walk around the pitch at the end and there were presentations made to the

retiring Peter Schmeichel and legendary striker Shaun Goater who was playing his last game for the Blues.

Marc Vivien Foe, the midfielder who sadly lost his life a few weeks later, also walked around waving to supporters probably not realising he was the last City player to score a goal at Maine Road some three weeks prior with a late strike against Sunderland.

After the players left, Manchester band Doves, all City supporters, took to the stage as did Badly Drawn Boy. Fireworks and ticker-tape brought an end to proceedings with many supporters lingering as long a possible for one last time.

City: Schmeichel, Dunne, Sommeil, Distin, Jensen, Wright-Phillips, Barton, Foe, Benarbia, Goater (capt), Anelka. Subs: Nash, Wiekens, Belmadi, Fowler, Horlock

54

The History of the Blues

Manchester City may have just moved into one of the greatest stadiums in the world, but their humble beginnings are a million miles from their new home at the City of Manchester Stadium. Formed as St Mark's of West Gorton, the early City team played their football on an area of rough ground in Clowes Street. The first recorded match was a 2-1 defeat to a team called Baptist Church of Macclesfield – both teams played with twelve players!

A year later, the name was changed to West Gorton (St Mark's) and three years after that they became Gorton.

Name, players and officials changed regularly around this time and in 1887 the new name was Ardwick with the club, such as it was, now playing at its fifth ground. It was around this time that an ideal venue was discovered for a home ground and Hyde Road became the destination for the early supporters to flock to.

After just seven years in existence, a financial crisis meant Ardwick had to change their name and from all the troubles, at last, the new club name of Manchester City F.C was born. City would continue to play at Hyde Road until 1923 by which time the venue had become decrepit and no longer matched the ambition of the club or its many supporters.

The decision was taken to move to a brand new purpose-built stadium in Moss Side and in August 1923, the Blues moved into Maine Road, designed to house 80,000-plus fans and be amongst the best

in the world. 58,159 fans witnessed the first home game – a 2-1 win over Sheffield United.

By this time, City were established as one of Britain's top clubs, having won the FA Cup in 1904 and been champions of Division Two three times and runners-up in Division One in 1921. The Blues then made three trips in eight years to Wembley to play in the FA Cup final, winning once (1934) and finishing runners-up on the other two occasions (1926 & 1933).

It wasn't until season 1936/37 that the Blues were crowned champions of England for the first time and the following season they became the first defending champions to be relegated! When you hear older people mutter "Typical City," it is because of such unbelievable chapters in their history!

The Second World War accounted for eight years of football in England and during this time City played in various regional leagues with teams made up largely of 'guest players'. By the time the war ended, there were many new faces in the side that had spent almost a decade in limbo in Division Two. The Blues wasted no time in storming to the title and winning promotion at the first time of asking with former skipper Sam Cowan in charge.

It wasn't until 1955 that City, now managed by Les McDowall, reached the FA Cup final again. They lost 3-1 to Newcastle but inspirational skipper Roy Paul vowed to return victorious the following year. True to his word, and just as City had done in 1934, the Blues returned to Wembley in 1956 to lift the trophy with a 3-1 win over Birmingham – in a game that City's goalkeeper Bert Trautmann broke his neck but continued playing!

The following years were barren for the club who were finally relegated in 1963 after a series of close escapes. After two years in the wilderness, Joe Mercer was appointed as manager and he employed young upcoming coach Malcolm Allison as his assistant. The results were dramatic as City won Division Two and, after just two years back in the top flight, were crowned champions of England for only the second time in their history.

The 'class of 1968' including many great players and the names of Colin Bell, Mike Summerbee, Francis Lee, Mike Doyle, Tony Book, Glyn Pardoe, Alan Oakes and Neil Young will be forever associated with the most successful period in the club's history. They won the FA Cup in 1969, the League Cup and European Cup Winners' Cup in 1970 by playing a brand of football that was exciting and entertaining to watch.

Things don't last forever and Joe Mercer left and Malcolm Allison took over briefly. It was the beginning of many managerial changes over the years but Tony Book's appointment in 1974 saw the club go on to League Cup glory in 1976 and finish runners-up in Division One in 1977. The last major cup final for City was the centenary FA Cup final in 1981 against Tottenham that the Blues lost 3-2 after a replay.

The 1980s were largely forgettable as the club bounced between the top two divisions and employed various managers along the way without any success. They steadied during the early 1990s and finished in fifth position for successive seasons in 1991 and 1992 but were relegated in 1996 to Division One and again in 1998, this time to Division Two, the lowest point in the proud history of the club.

The Blues missed automatic promotion at the first attempt but made the play-off final against Gillingham. Backed by around 40,000 City fans, the Blues trailed 2-0 with 89 minutes gone but incredibly fought back to draw 2-2 and win promotion through penalties. Manager Joe Royle then saw his side win a second successive promotion in 2000, finishing runners-up to Charlton Athletic.

Relegation followed in 2001 and former England manager Kevin Keegan replaced Royle as boss. City then stormed to the Division One title in 2002, breaking records for points, victories and goals along the way and returned to the Premiership for season 2002/03. The team, packed with world-class talent finished in ninth and qualified for the UEFA Cup via the Fair Play League to once again establish the club as one of the biggest in Europe.

They also moved into a new home after eighty years at Maine Road with the completion of the City of Manchester Stadium last summer. A new home, a great team and an inspirational manager - good times and trophies seem just around the corner again!

59

Club Honours

Football League (after 1992):
Division 1- Champions: 2001-2002
Runners up: 1999-2000
Division 2 - Play Off winners: 1998-99

Football League (before 1992):
Division 1 - Champions: 1936-37, 1967-68
Runners up: 1903-04, 1920-21, 1976-77
Division 2 - Champions: 1898-99, 1902-03, 1909-10, 1927-28, 1946-47, 1965-66
Runners up: 1895-96, 1950-51, 1988-89

FA Cup:
Winners: 1904, 1934, 1956, 1969
Runners up: 1926, 1933, 1955, 1981

League Cup:
Winners: 1970, 1976
Runners up: 1974

Full Members' Cup:
Runners up: 1986

European Cup Winners' Cup:
Winners: 1970

Charity Shield:
Winners: 1937, 1968, 1972
Runners up: 1934, 1956, 1969,1973

FA Youth Cup
Winners: 1986
Runners up: 1979, 1980, 1989, 2003

Central League
Winners: 1977-78, 1986-7, 1999-2000

AWARDS:
Football Writers Award
Don Revie 1954-55, Bert Trautmann 1955-56, Tony Book 1968-69 (shared with Dave Mackay)
PFA Young Footballer of the Year:
Peter Barnes 1976

Answers Page

Name Game

1. Eyal Berkovic
2. Nicolas Anelka
3. David Seaman
4. Joey Barton
5. Ali Benarbia
6. Michael Tarnat
7. Danny Tiatto
8. David Sommeil
9. Paulo Wanchope
10. Robbie Fowler

City Quiz

1. Shaun Goater
2. Birmingham City
3. Southampton & West Ham United
4. Nicolas Anelka
5. Darren Huckerby
6. Kevin Horlock
7. Marc Vivien Foe
8. Wigan Athletic
9. True
10. Matias Vuoso

City in Europe Quiz

1. Chelsea 0-2
2. True – League Cup and European Cup Winners' Cup in 1970
3. Gornik Zabrze – 4 times – once in 1970 and three times in 1971
4. Two – Juventus & AC Milan
5. True
6. They became the first side to visit the City of Manchester Stadium in a competitive game.
7. Joe Mercer, Tony Book & Kevin Keegan
8. None
9. Linfield – City scraped through on the away goals rule
10. Mick Channon

Who am I? Quiz

1. David Seaman
2. Paulo Wanchope
3. Jon Macken
4. Carlo Nash
5. Shaun Wright Phillips
6. Eyal Berkovic
7. Nick Weaver
8. Ali Benarbia
9. Nicolas Anelka
10. Kevin Horlock

Who said that?

1. Eyal Berkovic
2. Steve Howey
3. Peter Schmeichel
4. Sylvain Distin
5. Ali Benarbia
6. Paulo Wanchope
7. Jihai Sun
8. Robbie Fowler
9. Nicolas Anelka
10. Richard Dunne

True or False

1. True
2. False – he never played a first team game for United.
3. True – Southampton and Total Network Solutions are both known as The Saints
4. True
5. True – joint highest finish – same as 1993
6. True – City & PSG (blue), Real Madrid (white), Arsenal (red)
7. False – Robbie doesn't have a MBE – yet
8. True – v Stoke City in 1934 (84,569)
9. True
10. False – he was at Crystal Palace

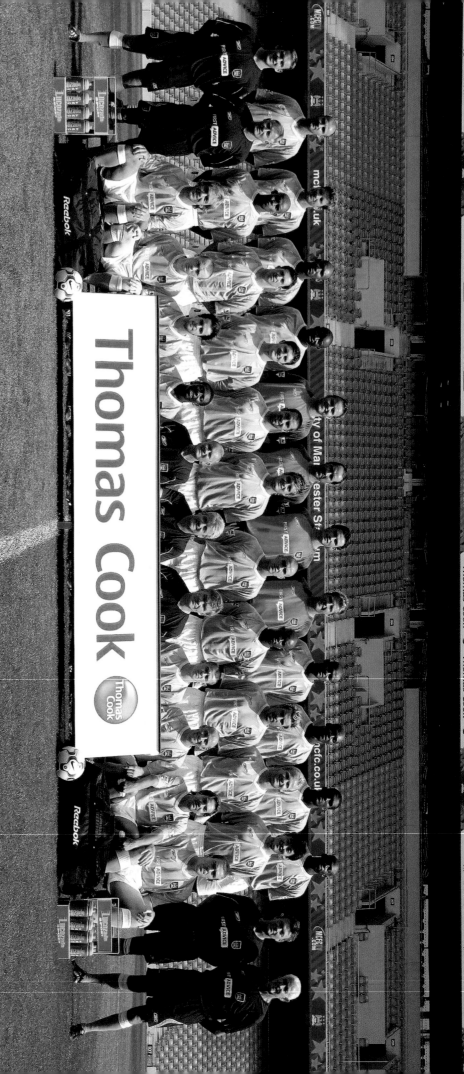